Jazzicle Pops!

Ten jazzy, bluesy & funky songs for children

CLASSROOM BOOKLET
Lyrics and recorder parts

Trixi Field

Second edition

Voice Confidence Publications

www.trixifield.co.uk
www.lulu.com/trixifield

Jazzicle Pops!

CLASSROOM BOOKLET

Trixi Field

All rights reserved. No part of this book may be reproduced or transmitted in any form or by any means, electronic or mechanical, including photocopying or recording or by any information storage and retrieval system without permission from the author, except for the inclusion of brief quotations in a review.

Original copyright © 2003
This edition © 2009 by Trixi Field

ISBN: 978-0-9559805-3-4

Cover design © 2008 Trixi Field
Cover photograph "Rock Singers" © 2008 Daniela Walter
(reproduced on the cover with the photographer's kind permission)

Contents

Lazy tune – lyrics	2
Lazy tune – descant recorder I	3
Lazy tune – descant recorder II	4
Lazy tune – descant recorder III	5
Mobile Phone Boogie – lyrics	6
Mobile Phone Boogie – descant recorder I	8
Mobile Phone Boogie – descant recorder II	10
The Sleepover Song – lyrics	12
The Sleepover Song – descant recorder	14
Bumble Bee Calypso – lyrics	16
Bumble Bee Calypso – descant recorder I	18
Bumble Bee Calypso – descant recorder II	20
How Can I Sing The Blues? - lyrics	22
Hero's Lullaby – lyrics	24
Hero's Lullaby – descant recorder	26
Song Train – lyrics	28
Song Train – recorder part	30
School Uniform Blues – lyrics	32
School Uniform Blues – descant recorder I	34
School Uniform Blues – descant recorder II	35
In The Hush – lyrics	36
In The Hush – descant recorder I	38
In The Hush – descant recorder II	40
I Can't Get My Aeroplane To Fly – lyrics	42

Lazy Tune

It's a mellow, lazy tune
Like a hazy afternoon
Voices sighing, voices low,
Lullabying, swinging, slow
It's a mellow, lazy tune
Like the soft and gentle moon.

Descant Recorder I

Lazy Tune

Gently rocking, like a lullaby ♩ = 130

Music & Lyrics by Trixi Field

Descant Recorder II

Lazy Tune

Gently rocking, like a lullaby ♩ = 130

Music & Lyrics by Trixi Field

Descant Recorder III

Lazy Tune

Gently rocking, like a lullaby ♩ = 130

Music & Lyrics by Trixi Field

Mobile Phone Boogie

Verse 1

When I'm upstairs in my room or up in a tree
I'll start in the morning and keep going till three
I'll do it in a bus and then I'll talk really loud
In a car, in a train or in the middle of a crowd
On my own, in a cave or down in a crater
I'll text you a message saying "C U L8er"!

Chorus 1

C U l8er, I'll C U l8er,
C U l8er, I'll C U l8er,
C U l8er, I'll C U l8er,
C U l8er, I'll C U l8er,
On my own, in a cave or down in a crater
I'll text you a message saying "C U L8er"!

Verse 2

I often like to start the day by texting a friend
Say "Hi" and " Howzit going XX" then press send
I'm never feeling lonely, no, I'm never alone
When I call my best friend on my mobile phone
I love to send a message or a text 2 U
Even though I'm sitting here right next 2 U.

Chorus 2

Next 2 U, right next 2 U,
next 2 U, right next 2 U
Next 2 U, right next 2 U,
next 2 U, right next 2 U
I love to send a message or a text 2 U
Even though I'm sitting here right next 2 U.

Descant Recorder I, page 1 of 2

Mobile Phone Boogie

Music & Lyrics by Trixi Field

Driving and Rumbustuous ♩ = 130

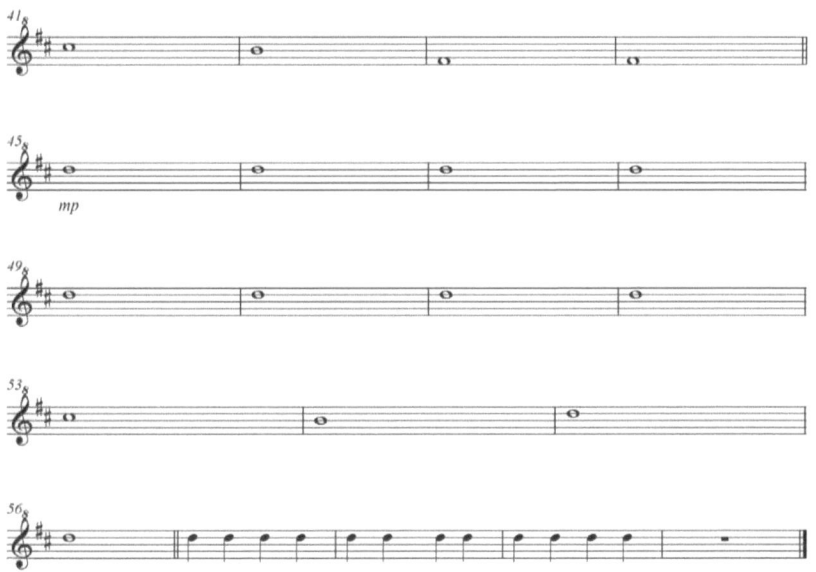

Descant Recorder II, page 1 of 2

Mobile Phone Boogie

Descant Recorder II, page 2 of 2

The Sleepover Song

Verse 1
Girls:
Emma and Jane and Nita are coming to sleep over tonight
We'll talk and eat and laugh and joke, and then we'll have a pillow fight
Tired in the morning, 'cos we won't sleep till one
It'll be fun.

Verse 2
Boys:
My sister and her schoolfriends are having a sleepover tonight
We'll put beetles in the sheets and bugs in the bed, and give them a massive fright

Girls:
Aaaargh!

Boys:

Tired in the morning, they'll fall asleep at school

It'll be cool

Girls:

Cool! Cool! Cool! Cool!

All:

Cool! Cool! Cool! Cool!

Cool!

Bumble Bee Calypso

Verse 1

I love summer but I hate the wasps
And I don't think the wasps like me
If I have to have a bug land on my nose
I'd rather it was a bumble bee

Chorus

'Cos the bumble bee is a teddy bear
He's big and fat and round
Yes, the bumble bee is all covered in hair
He's funny and fuzzy
With a bizzy buzzy sound.

Verse 2

The bumble bee is a cute little buggle
He's jolly and round and fat
If I were as small I would give him a huggle
But I can't, or else I'll squash him flat

Repeat chorus

Verse 3

He may not be stripey, he may not be yellow

But if a bumble you should spy

Spare a little thought for this jolly woolly fellow,

He may be a little lump but he can fly

Repeat chorus

Descant Recorder I, page 1 of 2

Bumble Bee Calypso

Descant Recorder I, page 2 of 2

Descant Recorder II, page 1 of 2

Bumble Bee Calypso

Descant Recorder II, page 2 of 2

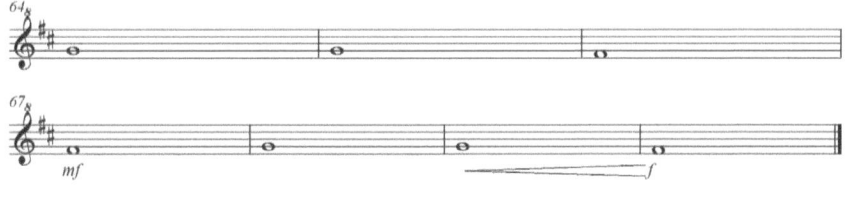

How Can I Sing The Blues

Verse 1

You can sing the blues when the skies are
dull and grey
You can sing the blues if you've had a horrid day
You can sing the blues if you can't go out to play

Chorus

I'm sad 'cos I'm happy and that just doesn't do,
If you're happy and you sing the blues, it won't sound true,
So how can I sing the blues if I ain't blue?

Verse 2

You can sing the blues if you're feeling down and out,
If you're lonely, angry, sad or full of doubt,
'Cos feeling sad is what the blues is all about

Repeat chorus

Verse 3

If you want to sing the blues you can't feel good,
I would sing about my sadness if I could,
But I don't feel half as rotten as I should

Repeat chorus

Hero's Lullaby

Verse 1

Here in my dreams I dive into the deep, ah, ah,
Being the hero whenever I sleep, ah, ah,
Saving a damsel or catching a thief
Floating to earth like a leaf
Until my clock starts to bleep,
And ends my deep sleep.

Verse 2

Here in my slumber I'm no longer me, ah, ah
Being what I've always wanted to be, ah, ah
Dolphin or butterfly, lion or mare,
Doing what I'd never dare,
Till my mum brings me some tea,
And gently wakes me

Verse 3

Wish I could stay and dream on through the day, ah, ah

Winter no more, just a long sunny May, ah, ah

Gliding or diving or being a star,

Driving a shiny red car

Till the sun's first golden ray

Brings a new day

Ah, ah, ah, ah.

Descant Recorder

Hero's Lullaby

Music & Lyrics by Trixi Field

Song Train

Verse 1

Come and join us here on the song train
We've got lots of room because it's a long train
We can give so much love to make it a strong chain
We'll roll all over the world singing our song, chugging along
Come on and join the song

Verse 2

Come and join us here on the song boat
There are lots of people here on our long boat
We can ride all the waves because it's a strong boat
We'll roll all over the world singing our song, floating along
Come on and join the song

Verse 3

Come and join us here on the song plane

If you want to fly, don't get on the wrong plane,

We can weather the storm because it's a strong plane

We'll fly all over the world singing our song, soaring along

Come on and join the

Come on and join the

Come on and join the song!

School Uniform Blues

Verse 1

I've got to wear my uniform when I go to school
I've got to wear my uniform when I go to school
But when the weekend comes and I'm home, well I look cool.

Verse 2

I've got some wicked jeans and a crazy pair of shoes
I've got some wicked jeans and a crazy pair of shoes
But then on Monday morning I get the school uniform blues.

Verse 3

Well I can't wait for the summer when there's no more black and grey
Well I can't wait for the summer when there's no more black and grey
Gonna wear green and orange and red and blue ev'ry day

Verse 4

Gonna wear lots of colour and dress just like the sun

Gonna wear lots of colour and dress just like the sun

Gonna be no more uniform, gonna have me some fun!

Oh yeah!

Descant Recorder I
School Uniform Blues

Jolly, with an end-of-term feel! ♩ = 140

Music & Lyrics by Trixi Field

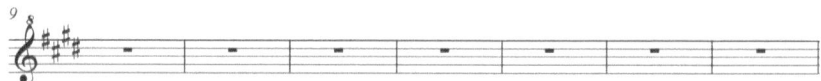

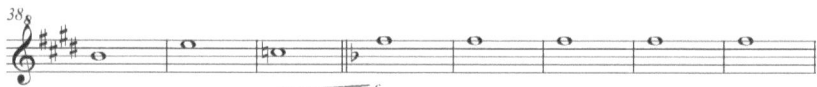

Descant Recorder II
School Uniform Blues

Jolly, with an end-of-term feel! ♩ = 140

Music & Lyrics by Trixi Field

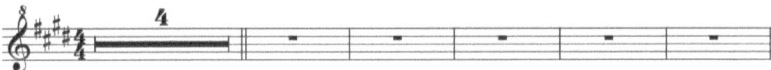

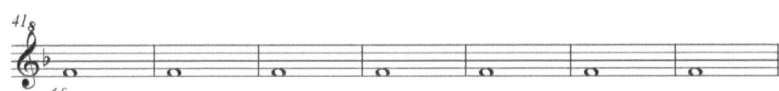

In The Hush

Verse 1

In the hush of the morning,
When the curtains are still drawn
We'll steal away to the edge of the seashore,
To watch the glow of the dawn.
In the silence just before sunrise,
Not a soul in sight
We'll watch the day unfolding,
Taking leave of the night.

Verse 2

When the day is a-dawning,
And the birds wake from their rest,
We'll steal away just to watch the horizon,
To see the sky at her best.
As the gulls start crying "it's morning!"
We'll go back to bed
And we'll pretend we stayed home,
Busy sleeping instead.

Verse 3

When the raindrops are falling,

And the day is dull and long,

Then we'll remember the edge of the seashore

And the early seagull's song.

When I'm sad, when I'm lonely,

Not a friend in sight,

Then I'll remember the seashore,

And the dawn's gentle light.

Descant Recorder I, page 2 of 2

Descant Recorder II, page 2 of 2

I Can't Get My Aeroplane To Fly

Verse 1

No matter how I try,

I can't get my aeroplane to fly

I've stuck a lot of bits on it

And a plastic pilot who sits on it

But however much I try,

I can't get my aeroplane to fly.

Verse 2

However hard I throw,

I can't get my aeroplane to go

I've tried adding extra wings

And other funny little whirly things

But no matter how I throw,

I can't get my aeroplane to go.

Verse 3

So even though I've tried,

My aeroplane won't glide

I've turned it into a little car

But still it won't go very far

And although I've tried and tried

It looks as though it died

'Cos it's landed on its side

And my aeroplane won't glide.

www.ingramcontent.com/pod-product-compliance
Ingram Content Group UK Ltd.
Pitfield, Milton Keynes, MK11 3LW, UK
UKHW041433180426
11947UKWH00007B/411